A POTPOURRI OF WORSHIP RESOURCES

Jeffrey T. Timm

A POTPOURRI OF WORSHIP RESOURCES

Copyright © MCMLXXVII by
The C.S.S. Publishing Company, Inc.
Lima, Ohio

All rights reserved. No portion of this book may be reproduced or utilized in any form or by any means, electronic or mechanical, including photocopying, without permission in writing from the publisher. Inquiries should be addressed to: The C.S.S. Publishing Company, Inc., 628 South Main Street, Lima, Ohio 45804.

ISBN 0-89536-198-1

PRINTED IN U.S.A.

To my parents and my wife Donna. Thanks goes to Gretta Kinman for all of her help with my manuscript.

TABLE OF CONTENTS

Introduction	7
Calls to Worship	9
A Prayer	15
Communion	17
Stewardship	22
A Time with Children	24
Camp Resource	29
Orders for Worship	32
Opportunities Sermon	35
Church and World Sermon	37
Youth Service	38
New Years Service	40
Camp Vesper Service	43
Differences Sermon	48
Sermon in Five Parts	49
First Person Sermons	52
How to Introduce Liturgical Dance	54
Valentine's Day Banquet	57
Advent Wreath	59
Chrismon Tree	64
Project Nativity	67
Hanging of the Greens	68
Christmas Birthday Party	71
Christmas Eve Service	75
Candlelight Service	79
A Christmas Prayer	83
Live Nativity	85
A Maundy Thursday Service	88
Live Last Supper	89
Lent Suggestions	95
Children's Easter Sermon	97
Benedictions	98

Introduction

Why is it that millions of Christians around the world gather weekly for worship? For some it is a matter of habit. Others do not give it much thought. Finally, there are those people who just cannot manage to put their purposes into words. It would appear that we are so conditioned that we do not stop to question what we are about as our congregations gather to worship I am sure that all would agree that they come to worship God. But what does that really mean?

For me the world and life are the grounds of worship. My purpose in life and in worship cannot be differentiated. Life and worship are the celebrations of God's presence and activity in the world. The sacred can come only out of the secular. This speaks of incarnational theology. Both are to be viewed as creations of God and as areas of his activity. Our lives are inseparable blendings of the sacred and the secular. This is said because we cannot segment ourselves to perform a purely sacred or secular function. Worship must be in the context of life.

My purpose in worship is built upon a discovery-expression model. The beginning of worship is to focus on God and to learn from him. This initial action is best described as Discovering — discovering who God is, who I am, and who we are as a Christian community. However, all of these discoveries neither happen in any one worship experience nor are they realized in a lifetime. Discovery is an on-going process which never comes to an end, for we never completely have a grasp on all of the "truth." Discovery begins with a mustard seed of faith.

Authentic worship must also speak of expression. Expression flows from discovery. We express our discoveries: who God is, who I am, and who we are as a Christian community. These three aspects of

Discovery-Expression are what worship is all about. They speak of life and call for growth.

Ultimately, as we discover and express, the conclusion is drawn that worship calls us to affirm and celebrate life. Revelation leads us toward discovering and expressing that: God is a God of love who acted and acts in our world, each person is a person of worth, and Christian communities are called to love.

Discovering and expressing cannot be an either/or proposition. These concepts are like the oars of a boat. Let the boat represent the Christian life. On one oar mentally paint the word "discover" and on the other oar the word "express." If you just pull on one oar you go in circles. Only when tension is placed on both does the boat begin to go straight.

Traditional worship has validity and is still meaningful to many persons, but there are also many other forms of worship which can be meaningful and authentically Christian. It is so disheartening to hear people say, "All we want you to do is preach the gospel." The gospel is all that we have to preach, but it needs to be understood that the gospel can be communicated in many ways and forms. It is my prayer that what follows will provide a few new and meaningful ways of Discovering and Expressing the Good News of Jesus Christ.

Calls to Worship

Minister: Greetings in the name of Jesus Christ.
People: Good morning.
Minister: This is our challenge: to find God as he is present with us; to listen for his still small voice; to allow him to be free; to come into his presence with the desire for growth.
People: We have come to grow through discovering and expressing.
Minister: Let us then begin our discovering and expressing as we come into God's presence through prayer and singing praises to his name.

Reader: Good morning.
People: Good morning.
Reader: Why have you come?
People: We have come to celebrate our lives in Christ and to praise God.
Reader: We believe in God who is love.
People: We believe in Christ who showed us what love can mean in our lives.
Reader: We believe in the Holy Spirit who is present among us.
People: We believe in faith as our trust in the never failing love of God.
Reader: We believe in hope which only a loving God makes possible.
People: We believe in meaning as a gift which becomes ours when we love and let ourselves be loved.
Reader: In order to love God, we must love one another.
People: In order to love one another, we must accept ourselves.
Unison: So, we believe in love as the only way of relating to God, to each other, and even to ourselves.
Reader: Let us sing of our love and joy in Christ.

EASTER

Leader: On this annual celebration of the first resurrection morn, Christian friends, where is the one place Christ is not?
People: You know the place. The Christ is not in the tomb. The Scripture affirms he is not here; he has risen just as he said. Come here and see the place where he lay.
Leader: Then, my family in Christ, where do we find him?
People: Alive! Luke records: "For forty days after his death he showed himself to them many times, in ways that proved beyond doubt that he was alive ..."
Leader: True! And the revelation of John says: "On the Lord's day the spirit took control of me, and I heard a voice ... Don't be afraid! I am the first and the last. I am the living one! I was dead, but look I am alive for ever and ever."
Unison: Amen and Amen.

GOOD NEWS

Trumpets: [Joust call]
Minister: Let the celebration begin! Let us put on the armor of God.
People: What should we put on?
Minister: "Have truth for a belt tight around your waist; then put on righteousness for your breastplate, and the readiness to announce the Good News of peace as shoes for your fee."
People: "We will at all times carry faith as a shield."
Minister: "And accept salvation for a helmet, and the word of God as the sword that the Spirit gives you."

People: With this armor we are now ready to celebrate the Christian life, and to come into God's presence with singing and assurance.

CHRISTMAS CALL

Minister: Let us gather to unite our lives in worship and prepare our hearts for the coming of Jesus.
People: Jesus came to our world many years ago. Now we will ask him to come into our hearts and live through our lives.
Minister: That leaves us with quite a challenge.
Unison: Come, Lord Jesus, into our hearts and kindle a fire of responsive love that we may know what it is to love and let you through us bring peace on earth.

GOOD MORNING

Minister: In a friendly way I ask "Who are you?"
People: We are described in many ways — as persons, by occupations, as husbands, wives, children, parents ...
Minister: But who do you say that you are?
People: We each see ourselves somewhat differently, but as we worship we anticipate that we shall see ourselves as sons and daughters of God — related to each other.
Minister: You say we have received life from God, and we are related to each other.
People: Yes, and in worship we look for ways by which we can make this specific in the life of each of us. Amen.

LENT

Minister: In the name of the Father and of the Son and of the Holy Spirit.
People: That is how we must begin.
Minister: God we open our hearts to you; we confess that we're not always ready for you; we confess we often fail to take you seriously; we confess that the joy of the Resurrection is often time turned to dullness by the smallness of our faith.
People: May you always be praised for you live in us in all our weakness. Help us to straighten out our beliefs and line them up with the cross and the empty tomb.

BROTHERHOOD THEME

Minister: RENEW: means being a new person in Christ — setting new goals — seeking new meanings for life in our time.
People: ENABLE: means trust God and others — putting our whole life into God's hands for his use in our time.
Minister: EXTEND: means accepting the world that God so loved and being the church in every part of our lives.
People: CELEBRATE: means being thankful to God for life, love, acceptance, forgiveness, redemption, and showing it in worship, witness, and service.
All: Each of us is a part of the whole church. We have something to be excited about as we RENEW, ENABLE, EXTEND, and CELEBRATE.

Minister: Good morning.
People: Good morning.
Minister: This is the beginning —

People: The beginning of what?
Minister: — of the hour, of friendships, of new thoughts, of new experiences.
People: — Yes, and the beginning of the rest of our lives.
Minister: Ok, let's begin by worshiping God.

Minister: Good morning.
People: Good morning.
Minister: It is good to be together again.
People: It is good in the midst of our work, talk, conflict, and resolution to come together to affirm both our separateness and our closeness — our humanity.
Minister: This is the day which the Lord hath made.
People: Let us rejoice and be glad in it.
Minister: The Lord be with you.
People: May he be with all of us.
Minister: Lift up your hearts.
People: Our hearts are already with the Lord.
Minister: We owe thanks to God.
People: Yes, it is only right to thank him and now celebrate the life he has given us.

Minister: Come, let us celebrate, let us kneel before the Lord our maker.
People: Let us sing his praises and listen to his word.
Minister: Have you walked the first mile of duty this week.
People: We have tried to do what was right.
Minister: Have you walked the second mile of love?
People: On occasions our footsteps have taken us the second mile once or twice and we have rejoiced in it.
Minister: Will you try to walk both miles next week?
People: With God's help we will try. Let us use these next moments to begin our journey.

Minister: Oh people, let us affirm our Lord, the meaning of our lives.
People: Let us affirm the life he wants of us.
Minister: Let us affirm our faith in that life, our faith in him.
People: We come to find his will in joy and celebration and to find him in the silence of our souls.

Minister: Good morning.
People: Good morning.
Minister: Welcome to this celebration of life in Jesus Christ.
People: We joyfully respond to him in worship.
Minister: Let us listen with our ears, see with our eyes, and be open in our mind.
People: We worship and praise you, O God, who makes every day new and all of life joyful.

Minister: We gather for worship in answer to God's invitation.
People: To exalt his name among men.
Minister: We gather through faith in Jesus Christ.
People: To keep our promise made unto him.
Minister: We gather in the power of the Holy Spirit.
People: To live as he directed.
Unison: "No one can deny how great is the secret of our religion! He appeared in human form, was shown to be right by the spirit, and was seen by angels. He was preached among the nations, was believed in the world, and was taken up into heaven." [1 Timothy 3:16]
Minister: In priase and thanksgiving, let us rejoice and sing.

A Prayer

Our Father and Our God,
It feels good to be here in your presence. We gather to praise your name and your works. We are thankful that your spirit is with us as we celebrate in this worship experience. May that spirit pervade our every thought and action.

Father, you gave us the beautiful gift of life, but we have misused that which you have given us.

You gave us eyes that we might see, yet we turn our vision inward. We fail to look beyond ourselves to our fellow man. When we see conditions that oppress we appear to be blinded. When we see conditions that require involvement, we turn away. Open our eyes to our world.

You gave us legs that we might move, yet we often do not move in the right fashion. We are like the people on the Jericho road who pass by their fellow man. Sometimes we are content not to move at all. We sit back and wait for someone else to move first. Move us in the right directions.

Father, you gave us hands, yet we are slow to extend them. We are slow to extend them toward our neighbor and toward you in prayer. We are hesitant to put our hands to work. Move our hands in new directions.

You gave us minds, yet we think too much about ourselves. We are slow to think about you and about others. Move us toward your purposes.

Father give us:
eyes that see our fellow man, feet that will carry us towards them, hands to work for them when we arrive, and minds that will motivate us towards the life that you showed us through your son, Jesus Christ. It is in that name that we ask this and every prayer.

Prayer response   "Let the Words of My Mouth"
Hallett

Communion

CALLS TO COMMUNION

This is a feast of remembrance and fellowship. All of Christ's followers are invited to partake of the loaf and cup, symbols of the life and suffering of our Master, and which sugests a spiritual union between Christ and his followers.

Come to this sacred table not because you must, but because you may, come not to testify that you are righteous, but that you sincerely love Jesus Christ and desire to be his disciples; come not because you are strong, but because you are weak; come not to express an opinion but to seek a presence and to pray for his spirit.

COMMUNION SENTENCES

Minister: As the emblem of commemoration and forgiveness are passed, may the love of God and the grace of our Lord Jesus Christ be with you.
People: And with you my brother.
Minister: Amen.

Elder: What shall I render to the Lord for all his goodness to me? I will lift up the cup of salvation and call on the name of the Lord: I will pay my vows to the Lord in the presence of all his people.
People: It is good to give thanks to the Lord; to sing praises to his name; to declare his steadfast love in the morning, and his faithfulness by night. The Lord has made me glad with his work; and for the work of his hand I sing for joy.

ELDER — PRAYER FOR EMBLEMS

Elder: In him there was life, and the life was the light of men. The light shines in the darkness, and the darkness has not overcome it.
People: The light that enlightens every man was coming into the world. And the word became flesh and dwelt among us, full of grace and truth; and we have beheld his glory.
Elder: Prayer for the emblems.

Elder: God's power has given us everything we need to live a godly life. In Jesus we are called to share in his glory and goodness.
People: Through Jesus we come to share in the divine nature. For this reason do your best to add goodness to your faith; and to your goodness knowledge; and to your knowledge, self control and godliness; to your godliness add brotherly love.
Elder: Prayer of Thanksgiving.

AN INVITATION

Minister: "Let a man examine himself, and so eat of the bread and drink of the cup." (1 Corinthians 11:28)
People: "Search me, O God, and know my heart! Try me and know my thoughts; and see if there be any wicked way in me, and lead me in the way everlasting." [Psalms 139:23]

ASSURANCE OF FORGIVENESS

Minister: "If we confess our sins, he is faithful and just, and will forgive our sins and cleanse us from all unrighteousness." (1 John 1:9)

People: "And if any man sin, we have an advocate with the Father, Jesus Christ, the righteous." [1 John 2:1]

This is the Lord's table. It matters not to which family of Christendom you belong. Come, for it is Christ who invites you.

COMMUNION

Hymn "Let Us Break Bread Together" (Verse 1)

Meditation

Breaking of Bread
  Minister: Ministering to you in the name of Jesus Christ I give you this bread which represents his body.
  Elder: Prayer over the loaf.

Distribution of Bread   Words of institution

Hymn "Let Us Break Bread Together" (Verse 2)

Pouring Wine
  Minister: Ministering to you in his name, I give you this cup which represents his blood.
  Elder: Prayer over the cup.

Distribution of Wine   Words of institution

Hymn "Let Us Break Bread Together" (Verse 3)

MEDITATION

We live in a country that many people consider the most advanced in the world. Our vast means of communication have played a large part in our growth. If we look at our world's problems we can also link this to communication ... or shall we say the lack of it.

The **generation gap** implies that old and young are having problems communicating.

Strikes all over the country tell us that labor and management are having their problems.

Our courts are filled with divorce cases where husband and wife can no longer communicate.

And isn't it the lack of communication that has caused us to send our troops to fight foreign wars?

It is at the Lord's table that this lack of communication comes to a stop. It is here that God clearly shows his love for us. Through his son's broken body. He also tells us, "He who eats of my body and drinks of my blood abides in me and I in him." So as you partake, won't you open up your heart and communicate with God?

COMMUNION MEDITATION FOR LENT

God does speak to us throughout the **Old Testament**. And he speaks to us right **here** where we **find ourselves**.

READ **Jeremiah 31:31-34**.

READ the words of Paul [**1 Corinthians 11:23-26**].

The "Old Covenant" was ratified in Moses day with a Blood Sacrifice; Paul shows that the death of Christ establishes a new covenant — fulfills prophecy — is a blood sacrifice on behalf of man — and freely given by God.

The liturgy of Passover recalls deliverance of the Jews from Egypt. The Lord's Supper recalls deliverance from sin. It confronts us with the love and holiness of Christ and his purpose in dying.

Paul's words call us to "Partake in Remembrance."
1. To look back at the life and work of Jesus.
2. To look forward — to his coming again.
3. To rejoice in his presence — to renew our fellowship. That is a theme of which Lent speaks. To rejoice as he is present in faith, present in prayer, and present as we find him in the elements, present as we allow him to be free in our lives.

All of this speaks of the New Covenant which Christ established for us. Calls us to make an individual response.

SMALL GROUP COMMUNION EXPERIENCE

1. Take a small roll and divide it evenly according to the number of people in your group.
2. Each person gives each of the group members a piece of his/her bread and says a word of appreciation for their contributions to the group.
3. Each person takes of the cup to symbolize his/her individual relationship with God.
4. End the experience with a passing of the peace or a hug.

Stewardship

Minister: What do you bring before the Lord?
People: We bring the common things of life: money, bread and wine, and self. We celebrate these gifts before their giver. We share them with each other and all our brothers. We seek God's spirit to bless them, and make of them a blessing to all whose lips and lives they touch; common things, by his grace, make miracles!

MEDITATION

We live in an age where information is readily available for most situations.

When our machines break down we can buy a repair guide to tell us how to get them running again.

When we buy a new gadget for our homes it always comes with instructions, telling us how to assemble it correctly.

When we go on a trip we take a road map to assist us in finding our way to that final destination.

When it comes to stewardship, however, we have overlooked that information that Jesus left us. He did say "If any man would come after me, let him deny himself and take up his cross daily and follow me." Self denial is part of Christian discipline. May there be that element of sacrifice in our giving. The directions here, like anywhere else, are of no avail unless followed. It is when they are followed that things begin to take the right shape.

STEWARDSHIP MEDITATION

There is an old story of the boy on his way to church school with two nickels which is still pertinent to our understanding of Christian stewardship. The boy had one nickel for church and one for candy. Along the way the boy dropped one of the coins and it rolled down into the sewer and couldn't be found. The boy went on his way saying, "Sorry, Lord, there goes your nickel." I pray that is not our response.

A Time with Children

Children can be the forgotten people of a worship service. Many times they come away from a worship service quite empty because the service has failed to make them feel that they are an important part of the community. Jesus was a master at sharing stories. He gave us the commission "to make disciples." The best place to start is right at home with the children of our community.

Let me suggest that this time not be a children's sermon, but rather a time with the children. Call the children forward and let them sit on the steps around you. The next step is to talk **with** the children. Let them answer and ask questions. Talking **at** them can at best be an extension of the sermon. Exciting things happen when children feel as if they have a meaningful part in the service. I am often surprised how this time speaks to the adults more than does the theological development of a sermon.

NO. 1

TOPIC: The Kingdom of God is like yeast.
Step 1: Read Luke 13:20-21
Step 2: Show the children some dry yeast.
Step 3: Place the yeast in water.
Step 4: Ask the children about how they understand the parable or if they have questions. Conclude with a few of your remarks.

NO. 2

TOPIC: Aids to See (take aids with you).
Step 1: Ask what the following aids help one to see.
   A: Mirror — self

B: Glasses — others
C: Binoculars — earth
D: Telescope — sky and other planets
E: Bible
Step 2: Conclude with your remarks.

NO. 3

TOPIC: The Gospel in a Nutshell.
Step 1: Give each child a hollow peanut with a slip of paper in it. On the paper have John 3:16 written out.
Step 2: Ask the kids if any of them know the verse and what does it mean to them.
Step 3: Conclude with your comments.

NO. 4

TOPIC: Mother's Day
Step 1: Ask the children what day it is. Ask the children to share some of the special things that mothers do.
Step 2: Read an appropriate Scripture.
Step 3: Give each child a flower and ask the kids to take it to their mother and to tell her they love her.

NO. 5

TOPIC: Christmas
Step 1: Ask: What is today? What is Christmas? What presents were left for you?
Step 2: This morning we are going to talk about people who came to the manger. Who came? How many wisemen came and what were their gifts? How many shepherds came?

Step 3: Tell the legend of the fourth shepherd who stayed behind.
Step 4: Teach the children to sing and then lead "We Wish You a Merry Christmas."

NO. 6

TOPIC: Faith.
Step 1: Put a jar of mustard seeds in a box and mark FAITH on the outside.
Step 2: Ask if there are any ideas about what is inside.
Step 3: Read a mustard seed Scripture.
Step 4: Ask once again if anyone can guess what is in the box.
Step 5: Show a picture of a mustard tree and talk with the children about faith.
Step 6: Give each child a mustard seed.

NO. 8

TOPIC: Being an Example.
Step 1: Draw a picture of a dog and tell the children that his name is Ralph. Ralph has a problem for which he is seeking pastoral counseling. You are wondering if the kids might help solve Ralph's problem. For years Ralph has owned all of the athletic equipment on his block. He has always decided what games the others would play even if it wasn't what they wanted. All of a sudden a new dog moved on the block with his own equipment. He allows the community of dogs to decide what they will do. Ralph says he no longer has any friends. What is Ralph's problem?
Step 2: Ask each child if he will take Ralph by an imaginary leash. They are to take him everywhere they go during the next week. Each child is to see if they can help Ralph solve his problem by their

example. Ask each child to take Ralph and to return to their pew.

NO. 9

TOPIC: Examples.
Step 1: Have the children report back their experiences from the previous week with Ralph.
Step 2: Read an appropriate Scripture and contribute some of your thoughts about their experiences.

NO. 10

TOPIC: Sharing.
Step 1: Read a Scripture about sharing.
Step 2: Ask the kids about ways that they share and ways that their parents share.
Step 3: Tell the kids that you appreciate their help and you want to give them a little reward. Give each child two pennies. Be sure that you run out of pennies and one child gets no reward.
Step 4: See how the kids respond and deal with the situation as it develops.

CHILDREN'S CREATIVE ACTIVITY

Why not use the back of your bulletin for a children's creative activity? It is easy to make up puzzles based on Scripture passages. This might allow the children to sit still so that the parents can listen to the sermon. It would also allow the child to be involved in studying the Bible.

Example: Unscramble the Names found in Matthew 10:2-4:

SDUAJ.................................
DASEAUHDT ....

EMSJA................................
RNAWDE...............................
ETPRE................................
HJNO.................................
LEMOWTRABOH..........................
LIPHPI...............................
MAJES................................
NISMO................................
HSAMOT...............................
WHATEMT..............................

Camp Resources

3 - 4 DAY CAMP OR RETREAT EXPERIENCE

Camp Theme: "I Believe"

Times: Arrive just before supper on Monday and leave after lunch on Friday.

Group: Junior and Senior High Youth. Each group meets separately for Session 1 and 2.

Schedule:

7:15-7:45	Wake and Shine
7:45-8:00	Morning Devotions by the Youth
8:15-8:45	Breakfast
9:00 - 10:30	Session 1
11:00 - 12:30	Session II
12:45 - 1:30	Lunch
1:30 - 5:00	Free time
5:00 - 6:00	"Different mini-programs"
6:15 - 7:00	Supper
7:30 - 9:00	Evening Program (fun activities)
9:00 - 10:30	Free time
10:30 - 11:00	Night Watch (counselors)
11:30	Lights out

Tip: We might have found a way around camp pranks. We make an agreement that all pranks would wait until 5:00 Thursday. At that time we put in an open field everyone who chose to participate and let them go at it. The results were wild!

Topics:
   Tuesday: God
   Wednesday: Jesus
   Thursday: Christian Life
   Extra Day: Holy Spirit

Evening Programs:
   Movies - Banners
   Bingo
   Talent Night
   Square Dance

We based our camp experience around the theme "I Believe." On the first evening each camper was given a sheet that contained various examples of affirmations of faith. This was just to give the camper an idea of what was expected. After returning the sheet, which was returned to the camper at the end of camp, we asked each camper to write what he/she believed in the form of an affirmation. For many this was a near impossible task. We then explained the camp theme and that our goal was another affirmation of faith at the end of camp. This affirmation was to reflect where each person was in his/her thinking at the end of the camp experience. These affirmations were collected, reproduced, and shared with all. I think the following affirmations will reflect that much growth was realized through our camp experience.

   I believe that the Lord God is a true God and that he sent his only son down to earth to die for our sins and through him we may have eternal life in his kingdom. I believe that God is the world's creator. That he made man in his own image. I believe that he will give me clothes and drink when I need them. I believe that both God and Jesus Christ are **love**.

   I believe that he is mighty and understanding, and does not despise any.

   I believe that God is my light and the light of the world for us to follow and there is no darkness in him. I believe that God is God and that he is good. A God who knows all things. I believe that Jesus Christ was with God in the beginning and will always be with him until the end. I believe without him there would be nothing. I believe that God has a plan for my life and yours until the end

I believe that God loves all his creation. I believe in the Bible! I believe that he will come for us all at the end. He is my only God and I don't think he would mean all these things to me if I did not believe.

I believe that God is our Father, the one who created all things. I believe in Jesus Christ, son of God, who is our personal Savior and our only hope for salvation. Through believing, trusting, and putting our faith in him, we can acquire eternal life. I believe that through Jesus Christ's name God will forgive us of our sins but only if we forgive others first and truly mean what we pray. I believe that through honest and meaningful prayers God will answer our prayers in the way he sees best, and show us the path that he wants us to follow. I believe that the Holy Spirit is with us always to guide and guard us through whatever we come across. I also believe that through his undying love for us we can learn to love our fellow neighbor and spread the good and wonderful news that God is still alive and living in many hearts.

I believe in an all-powerful and all-knowing God, who created the universe and everything in it. I believe he is a God of Love, and that this love is manifested in his Son, Jesus Christ, who sacrificed himself for my sins. I believe Christ is the only way to a relationship with God, and only through him are we offered forgiveness for all our sins and eternal life. I believe that through conversation with God, talking and listening, we can grow closer to God and he will answer our prayers by doing what is best for us. I believe the Bible is the inspired Word of God, and by studying it we can learn more about who God is and what he wants us to be like. I believe that the Holy Spirit dwells within me, and that only by being filled and empowered by him are we able to live the true Christian life. I believe that God can work all things out for good so he should be praised for all things, good and bad.

Orders for Worship

Words should say exactly what you want them to say. Does your bulletin speak for you? If not, let me suggest the two following orders for worship.

ORDER FOR WORSHIP #1

Welcome to our worship service. As you quietly wait for the service to begin, we encourage you to reflect upon why you are here, what you desire, and what you expect. Then give this to God in silent prayer and allow him to come to you as you come to him.

Organ Prelude

Focusing on God — Beginnings for Worship (Call)

Calling for God's Presence (Invocation)

The Hymn of Gathering

Welcome and concerns of our community

Special Music

A time with the children

23rd Psalm (In unison)

The Gloria Patri

The Good News

Choral Call to Prayer

Pastoral Prayer and the Lord's Prayer

Choral Amen

Stewardship Hymn   "We Give Thee But Thine Own"
                                        (Verses 1 and 2)

Bringing Our Gifts to God

The Anthem Presentation and Praise to God (Doxology)

A Prayer of Dedication

Hymn

Sermon

Hymn of Dedication

Benediction

The Great Amen — Amen, Amen, Amen, Amen, Amen

Postlude

ORDER FOR WORSHIP #2

Welcome to this service of worship. "This is the day which the Lord has made; let us rejoice and be glad in it." That is quite a challenge for each of us. May these moments, that we have together as a community, be used as a springboard towards reaching that goal. Now is a good time to begin.

PROLOGUE

PREPARATION
    The Organ Prelude
    Focusing on God — Beginnings for Worship

The Invocation
Hymn of Preparation
Welcome and concerns of our community
A time with the Children

THE SITUATION
A Responsive Reading
The Gloria Patri
The Good News

THE DEDICATION
Concern
- Call to Prayer
- Pastoral Prayer
- Lord's Prayer
- Choral Amen

Commitment
- Offering Hymn
- Stewardship thought
- Bringing Our Gifts to God
- Anthem
- The Presentation and Doxology
- A Prayer of Dedication

WITNESS TO THE GOOD NEWS
Hymn of Challenge
Sermon

EPILOGUE
Hymn of Dedication
The Benediction
The Great Amen
The Postlude

Opportunities Sermon

This is a sermon where experiences preach. Two people are needed for this dialogue sermon. You might want to put the following statement in your bulletin: In our time Christians are finding value in traditional forms of worship, but they are also searching for new ways of rediscovering and communicating the Good News. Today's "sermon" is an attempt to experience, in a fresh way, the opportunities that are for Christian growth. This morning's "sermon" will be a dialogue.

The pulpit will not be used at all for this experience. Begin this experience by having a weekend golfer enter from the side door with a putter. Let him spend fifteen to twenty seconds practicing his putting stroke. The golfer then greets a church member on his way home from church. They engage in conversation that leads to questions about what the church member's church, your church, has to offer. At this point have the two men pull out lawn chairs from behind the pulpit and lectern. Finish the dialogue from the lawn chairs.

The background setting is: a man who has dropped out of going to church several years ago, but still goes on holidays like Easter and Christmas. He is a very avid weekend golfer. However, the golfer is worried about his family's spiritual life. This drop-out is engaged by one of your members who is trying to get the golfer interested in his (your) church. This is a good way to talk about what your church or chapel offers as opportunities for growth. You might consider this experience for early September.

Let me suggest a starting place.

Golfer: Hi, looks like you have been to church.
Member: Sure have. I wish you would join me some Sunday.
Golfer: I would but this is my only day to play golf. Besides I kind of have a private form of religion.

(Pause) Well, I guess if I am honest I must confess that I am worried about my spiritual life and that of my family. What does your church have to offer me?
Member: Well, what are you looking for?
Golfer (looks at watch): I have about fifteen minutes before I have to go; let's pull out a couple of chairs and talk if you have time.
Member: I always have time to talk to someone about my church.
Golfer: What am I looking for? I am looking for a church where we can grow in our faith. I want to be part of a church that makes a difference in people's lives. A church which will challenge me.

At this point I leave you on your own. I would, however, suggest the following areas:
1. Growth opportunities — Sunday School, Bible Studies, Worship
2. Expression — choirs, Christian Education
3. Fellowship
4. A church that matters — Service projects
5. Challenges

You may want to conclude by saying that the church is people. Christians are god's people in the world. The two "preachers" may want to conclude by inviting the congregation to participate in the opportunities that are offered by your church. This would be a good time to invite members to this evening's church supper.

Church and World Sermon

When it is time for the minister to preach he should go stand between the lectern and pulpit. At this time the organist should begin to play the wedding march. A boy and girl will enter from the back and proceed down the main aisle. Around the girl's neck is a sign with "Church" written on it. Around the man's neck is a sign with "World" written on it.

The minister reads the wedding service, excluding the giving away of the bride, until he says, "Therefore, if any man can show just cause why they may not be lawfully joined together, let him now speak, or else hereafter forever hold his peace." At this point you need to have a plant in the congregation who will stand up and object to the marriage. The minister then says, "Church and World, will you have a seat in the first pew, and perhaps we need to look at the situation."

Charles L. Wallis' 1976 Minister's Manual has an excellent sermon, on page 195, for this experience. Your sermon should challenge the people to be confronted with the answering of your original question.

Youth Service

The theme of this service is Day by Day. Make your own bulletin covers and then let the children color them for the congregation. Why not decorate the hallway so as to create some expectancy? I would suggest a large eye, a large heart, and a long pathway.

Organ Prelude

Bringing in the Light (Two youth with candles in hand enter and light the sanctuary candles from their candles.)
Youth #1: Jesus is the light of the world.
Youth #2: So, let your light shine also.

Call to Worship

Hymn of Celebration   "I Believe in Jesus"
(Sung to "I Believe in Music.")

Invocation

Contemporary Lord's Prayer

Gloria Patri

The Greeting

Call to Prayer
Minister: The Lord be with you.
People: And with thy spirit.
Minister: Let us pray in a new and different way.

Pastoral Prayer by Music   "Day by Day"
Youth Band

A Responsive Reading

Hymn of Experience "Amazing Grace"
(Sung to the tune of the Coke Song)

Messages:
  Number One — To see thee more clearly.
  Number Two — To love thee more dearly.
  Number Three — To follow thee more nearly.

Interpetive Dance to Day by Day

Communion Meditation

Presentation of Gifts (Worshipers will come forward at the request of the ushers, leave their offering in the plates provided on a table at the front of the chancel steps.)

Sharing the Elements (Worshipers go to the communion table.)

The Visible Community (From the communion table the worshipers will follow the ushers directions in forming a circle around the sanctuary.)

Pass It On (Pass a sentence to each side, and each person will pass it to the person next. Two messages, such as God is love, will be going around at the same time. When they return to the minister he should declare the messages.

Hymn "Blest Be the Tie That Binds"
(Verse 1)

Benediction

Taking Out the Light (The two youth light their candles from the altar candles.)
Minister: Take your light into the world. Go now in peace.

New Year's Service

Begin the evening at 8:00 with games, a dance, and pizza making. The first order of busines is to decorate the party place. At 11:30 all the worshipers should move into the sanctuary.

On the altar have twelve lighted candles. Give twelve youth call to worship Scriptures. You will also need a burned, short candle and a sleek new candle on the altar. The service begins in darkness. Lights should go on with the beginning of the litany response.

Music Prelude

Beginnings for Worship — This is the new year which the Lord has made, let us rejoice and be glad in it.

Lighting of the Worn Candle — We light this worn down candle to remind us that the old year is quickly coming to an end.

The Twelve Candles — The twelve lighted candles represent each of the twelve months of the past year. They represent the past and symbolize the expectancy of a new year.

A Message — "Declare his glory among the nations, his marvelous works among all the peoples."

Twelve Scripture Calls (One candle is put out with each call.)

Invocation:
Almighty God and most merciful Father, who has given us grace in times past, and has mercifully brought us to see the end of another year: Grant that we may continue to grow in grace and in knowledge of your Son Jesus Christ. Lead us forward by your

spirit that we may better serve you in the year to come. In this new year undergird us in our faith that we may see you more clearly, love you more dearly, and follow you more nearly in 19 . Grant this our prayer, O Gracious Father, which we offer in the name of Jesus Christ. Amen.

A Litany (Lights)
Minister: God calls us to continue our celebration as we come to worship. We gather as a community of faith in light of the new year which lies ahead. A year in which God will be our guide.
People: HAPPY NEW YEAR.
Minister: We come with joy and hope, praise and thanksgiving. Expectancy is ours because we face this new year together as a community of faith. A community that has potential to make a difference. A community which celebrates the Good News of Jesus Christ. Our help is in the name of the Lord.
People: HAPPY NEW YEAR.
Minister: The old year is behind us now, the new year lies ahead of us. To the old we say farewell, to the new we say hello. Let us celebrate this future with words of welcome.
People: HAPPY NEW YEAR.

Hymns   Your favorites

New Year's thought
   1. Where are you going?
   2. What is your cargo?
   3. Who is your pilot? Questions asked boats in NY harbor.

Light new candle from the old:
This new candle represents that new year which comes out of the old. A year which will be what you make of it.

Benediction:
Phillips Brooks: "Life is full of ends, but every end is a new beginning, and we are continually coming to the point where we close one chapter; but we always can turn and open a new and better and a divine chapter."

Scripture Calls for New Year:
Each Scripture is on a 3 x 5 card that can be handed out.
1. Our help is in the name of the Lord, who made heaven and earth.
2. Revelation 21:5
3. Revelation 3:8
4. Psalms 90:12
5. Ezekiel 18:31
6. Sing unto the Lord a new song, his praises from the end of the earth.
7. Psalms 90:1,2c
8. God will be our guide forever
9. John 1:14
10. Come let us walk in the light of the Lord, that he may teach us his ways and that we may walk in his paths.
11. James 4:8
12. Isaiah 40:3

Camp Vesper Service

A camp vesper service allows for youth participation. This service is best suited to a dark room or for an evening service. All of the symbols, signs, and stations can be designed by the youth. At least nine youths with flashlights are needed. You will need nine stations spread around your setting. The setting is completely dark. The reader begins by reading the script from the back of the setting. At the marked points a youth will put his light on the featured station. One youth should be seated close to each station. When the next station is featured the previous light goes off. At the conclusion, all are lighted. It might be meaningful to conclude with a communion service.

A CAMP VESPER SERVICE

And then looking around on that little group of men very near to his heart, so soon to be deprived of his physical presence, even his clothes would be the property of the crucifixion squad of soldiers (Sandals), there was one thing he could give: "Peace I leave with you, my peace I give to you" — a mighty gift indeed. "Not as the world gives do I give to you". What does he mean by this? In those days the ordinary salutation at the end of a meeting or a greeting to a passer-by was "Peace be with you." (Peace Sign) But as the meaningful ancient prayer which we use — "May God be with you" has been shortened to "good-by" which now-a-days means little more than I must be going so in the world of man the peace they flung around had little significance.

Christ was going away but the peace he offered his disciples was real and well worth gaining.

My peace he says:

"Trust God wholeheartedly, as I have trusted and do

trust him; accept unquestioningly his ordering of your life; lay your whole being at his absolute disposal, holding back nothing, making no reservations, and you will have a peace that passes understanding garrisoning your heart; and you will come through with honor and in quietness of spirit — calm, steady and unafraid. (God is Peace)

Too many feel that the road to peace runs through self indulgence and satisfying one's passions and desires.

So Christ ends by repeating the rally cry with which he began: "Let not your hearts be troubled, neither let them be afraid."

He gave then a real and many sided encouragement that though unseen, he would be working for them in the other world (Earth), that they now knew God as he really is and could trust him utterly; that though they were about to scatter and fail tragically, they might not lose heart about themselves for he himself trusted them and was sure they would do his works.

1. They had in their hand the gift of prayer. (Prayer)
2. That they have the Holy Spirit as their counselor that led by him farther and farther into all the truth.
3. That Christ himself would make his hope with them, he and the Father.
4. That if they would believe all that and walk in the strength of it they would have his peace to steady them and bring them through with honor.

The legacy of Jesus is not trouble but peace. He doesn't council peace, he gives it! How unlike the superficial talk of peace on men's lips. Where this peace dwells there can be no foolish regrets and misgivings not even sorrow at the words of farewell and promise.

Peace, what a treasure! — (Treasure Chest)

He that has abiding peace is rich indeed. Multitudes are seeking peace, but fail to find it for peace can never be gained by personal effort. It is a gift of God, to be received through Jesus Christ. "My peace I give to you," the Master says to every believing soul.

Let us observe that it is his peace which he offers. Since he redeemed us from death by dying in our stead, he can say to every repentant sinner: "Be of good cheer, thy sins are forgiven thee" and since he is the Son of God he is able to save us in the storms of life saying: "Peace be still" until we know in life the gladness of "a great calm." — Pause —

Have we this heavenly peace?

Or, are we still among earth's anxious millions? Peace is what we need to make us:
1. Happy
2. Rich
3. Secure

Let us take Christ at his word: Yes, take Christ himself as our own personal Saviour and we will have perfect peace — life's greatest treasure.

"Blessed are the peacemakers: For they shall be called the children of God." (Matthew 5:9-12)

So said the great Peacemaker who came to bring that of which Bethlehem's angels sang: "Peace on earth, good will to men." (STAR)

International agreement can't establish peace until the approach is made in spirit of the Prince of Peace.
1. Malice towards none.
2. Charity for all.

To have peace with our fellowmen we must first be at peace with God through Christ who said: "Peace I leave with you, my peace I give unto you." (SMALL CROSS AND SILHOUETTE)

This peace belongs to the believing children of God. It can't be taken away or destroyed by:
1. Persecution.
2. Death.

The emphasis on peace and peacemaking is frequent in the teaching of Jesus. It was fitting that on his birth the angels sang "Peace on earth."

He said:
1. Love your enemies

2. Do good to them that hate you.
3. Pray for them that despitefully use you.

Peace is reconciliation with God. Jesus Christ is the prince of peace, peace in the soul and peace among men. His age was torn as is ours, with strife and hatred. In all ages nations are at odds, trade and home are torn by strife, and the individual's soul is alienated from God.

It was only by his death on the cross that all mankind was given an open path to peace. (BIG CROSS — if possible behind a door that is opened)

Jesus tells us; Behold I stand at the door and knock, if any man hear my voice, and open the door, I will come in.

Peace which passeth all understanding shall keep your hearts and mine through Jesus Christ.

47

Differences Sermon

Put a large sheet of posterboard in the front of the church. Magic marker needs to be in easy reach.

At the beginning of the sermon take time to ask each person in the congregation to come forward and make his or her mark. When the last few people are making their mark, the minister should go to the back of the church. At the conclusion of the marking the minister can comment about the marks. You might be aware of:
1. How different each is.
2. How some marks are in the middle, some in the corners alone, and that there are those clustered around others.
3. How some marked over others.
4. How some cooperate with others.
5. How some formed little groups.

The minister can now start back towards the pulpit as he continues to comment. When he arrives at the pulpit he may want to take the opportunity to preach about community or how God loves us as different as we all are.

"GOD IN A BOX"

Put a box on the pulpit that has GOD written on all six sides. Be sure and have at least one side that will open. Call one of the children forward and ask him to open the box. Then ask him what he sees. After it is determined that there is nothing in the box and the child is reseated, throw the box down.

The opportunity is now available to preach on putting God in a box. The minister may also want to deal with Paul's conviction that God is not only found in sanctuaries of men.

Sermon in Five Parts

*The Prelude

*The Chiming of the Hour

*The Call to Worship

*The Invocation

*The Hymn of Praise
    Minister: (Jeremiah 32:17) Ah Lord God! It is thou who hast made the heavens and the earth by they great power.
    Congregation: With men this is impossible but with God all things are possible.
    Minister: (Psalms 51:10) Create in me a clean heart, O God, and put a new and right spirit within me.
    Congregation: [Hebrews 12:28] Since we have been given a kingdom that is unshakeable, let us serve God in ways that please him, but always in reverence and thankfulness.

The Greeting

The Anthem

The Scripture Lesson

Unison: James 5:13-16

The Sermon, Part I   "The Singing Church" Minister

*The Hymn of Fellowship   Congregation

The Sermon, Part II   "The Healing Church" Minister

The Silent Meditations   Congregation

The Sermon, Part III "The Praying Church" Minister

The Hymn of Prayer Congregation
    Minister: The Lord be with you.
Congregation: And with they spirit.
    Minister: Let us pray.

The Pastoral Prayer Minister

The Choral Response Choir

The Sermon, Part IV "The Forgiving Church" Minister

The Communion Hymn Congregation

The Prayer of Thanksgiving for the Loaf Minister

The Prayer of Thanksgiving for the Cup Minister

The Fellowship of Communion
    Minister: As the emblems of commemoration and forgiveness are passed, may the love of God and the grace of our Lord Jesus Christ be with you.
Congregation: And with you, my brother.
    Minister: All those who acknowledge Jesus as the Christ have his invitation to share in his memorial feast. Please hold the loaf and the cup for unison paticipation.

The Sentence of Inaugural for the Loaf Elder

The Sentence of Inaugural for the Cup Elder

The Offering Sentence Minister

The Reception of Tithes and Offerings Deacons

*The Doxology Congregation

The Sermon, Part V   "The Concerned Church" Minister

*The Hymn of Invitation   Congregation
   As we sing this hymn, those desiring to make the Good
   Confession that Jesus is the Christ, and those wishing
   to unite with the church by transfer of membership
   are invited to step forward and be received by the
   minister.

The Benediction   Minister

*The Choral Response   Choir

*The Postlude   Organist

First Person Sermons

A very effective preaching tool is to use an occasional first person sermon. My first knowledge of the possibilities of first person sermons came from an excited layperson. My fraternity house-mother returned from an evening service in 1970, raving about the first person sermon her pastor had delivered. She told how meaningful and educational the experience had been for life. I requested a copy from her pastor. Some three years later I tried out the sermon. The results were outstanding. Many commented that the first person sermon was the most unique experience they had ever had in a worship service. I really felt that I had challenged people in a way that I had never challenged before.

The experience can be started by reading Luke 22:1-6. Then have two youth help you act out the situation. The youth will play the part of the priest and guard. After they talk about the details they should bring you to a table in front of the pulpit, to make arrangements for betrayal of Jesus. Leave the table with a bag of silver and go to the pulpit. Let me suggest a beginning and an outline.

Good morning, perhaps many of you recognize me. My name is Judas Iscariot. I was one of the twelve disciples of Jesus, the carpenter of Nazareth. I have been granted the opportunity of speaking out of the first century to you in the 20th because I have been misjudged by a majority of the historians and I simply want to set the record straight. I will make no attempt to vindicate myself. I am known throughout Christendom as Judas the betrayer. They even name all betrayers after me — Judas. I cannot change that record. The misunderstanding has come at the point of the **reason** for my betrayal, not the fact of it. Let me begin at the beginning.

1. Birth, and history of the name Judas
2. Judas' parents
3. Judas' experiences as a disciple
4. Betrayal — why
5. Judas' feelings about the arrest and crucifixion
6. Judas betrayed not because he ceased to love Jesus — but because he failed to understand.

How to Introduce Liturgical Dance

Liturgical dance is a new experience for most communities. The hardest service is always the first. Most people will have some reservation about the first time dance until it becomes a happening in their church. Your big problem will be locating a person who is willing and able to incorporate dance into your worship service. My experiences with incorporating liturgical dance into the worship service have been some of the most meaningful of my ministry. Dance has the unique ability of being able to create all kinds of expectancy. If this expectancy can be channeled, then meaningful things can happen.

Let me suggest the following service for your first venture. It shows the evaluation of man's expression. Dance is part of that expression.

"MAN'S EXPRESSIONS OF PRAISE"

Prelude

Chiming of the Hour Praise by Sound, Praise by Voice

Call to Worship

The Lord's Prayer

Man Communicates Minister

A Greeting People communicate a welcome to each other

The Scriptures Speak Psalms 149

Responsive Minister, odd verses
Congregation, even verses
Praise through Responsive Joy

Simple Expressions   Minister
"Greensleeves" on organ

Advancing Group Expression   Minister

Hymn

Advanced Expression   Minister

Anthem

Call to Prayer
    Minister: To thee, O Lord, I make my suplication.
    People: O Lord, be thou my helper. Hear, O Lord, and be gracious to me.
    Minister: Thou hast turned my mourning into dancing
    People: O Lord my God, I will give thanks to thee forever.

Pastoral Prayer

Choral Response

An Affirmation of Commitment

Offering — Doxology

Praise through the Sacrament of Communion

A Communion Proclamation

An Anthem of Christian Unity   "They will know we are Christians by our Love"

Psalm 150: 1-4a

An interpretative dance done to: Reading of "Lord of the dance" or to piano.

Breaking of Bread

Pouring of Wine

The Distribution — Words of Consecration

Hymn "Blest Be the Tie"

A Corporate Benediction

The Choral Response

The Postlude

Valentine's Day Banquet

Valentine's Day is a good time to gather your community together. Why not have a Sweetheart Banquet? Following is a suggested order for an evening of fun.

...Our lives are shaped by those who love us ... and by those who refuse to love us.
...I feel the capacity to care is the thing which gives life its deepest significance . . . (Casals)
...Unless you love someone, nothing else makes any sense . . . (Cummings)

Welcome, "Lovers." It is a great tragedy that the description of a person as a "great lover" implies degrading and derogatory overtones. Now that is a shame! In all of God's creation, only human beings can love, and herein lies our uniqueness and greatness. Tonight we affirm ourselves as "lovers."

A SPECIAL VALENTINE MESSAGE

I love you.
I want to give you some presents
that will delight your heart.
I have for you light and life, hope,
forgiveness and real freedom.

I am the source of all things
you long for and need
and can't get by yourself.
I have high hopes for you —
I sent Jesus to show you.
He offered his life freely for you.
He is lasting satisfaction.
He seeks you and wants you.
Don't be afraid or proud. Come:
Receive him wholly into your life.
Love him as your Lord.

Love others as I love them.
Care for all their needs,
and you will be complete.

I love you and want you
to know and be assured in all
that is good, right, and perfect,
So please be mine.

All my love,
God

Be it as friends, marital partners, or parents. As "lovers," let us be the happiest, warmest, and most caring people on God's earth this night. Let us experience and celebrate what being a "lover" is in the truest and best sense.

A Welcome to Lovers and a History of Valentine's Day

A Banquet for Lovers

Some Fun for Lovers Presented by some Steeple People

Some Oldies but Goodies ...   Songs, that is

Barber Shop Quartet   (The "tired" Lovers)

A Lovers Sing-A-Along

A Renewal Time for Lovers   The Oldest Staff Lover

A Lovers Program Ends ...But...Love Never Ends

Sing-A-Long Songs

Advent Wreath

During the past several centuries, the four weeks prior to Christmas have been observed by Christians as a time of spiritual preparation for the coming of Jesus. This four week period has taken on the name Advent. Our word Advent comes from the Latin word, "Advenio," which means "to come."

Advent is a season of expectancy and preparation. Expectancy causes us to look forward to the climax of the season of Advent—Christmas. Preparation calls us to be ready when Christmas arrives. Purple is the liturgical color for the Season of Advent.

There are several ways to help your congregation with their expectancy and preparation. The following resources are designed to aid your journey through Advent.

THE ADVENT WREATH

On the first Sunday and each succeeding Sunday of Advent, a candle in the Advent Wreath is lighted as a sign of spiritual preparation for the coming of Christ.

SYMBOLISM OF THE ADVENT WREATH

The Circle — with no beginning and no end, stands for the eternity of God.

The Evergreen — represents life and growth.

Four Candles — represent the four Sundays of Advent; the time of preparation.

Purple — the liturgical color for Advent stands for penitance and symbolizes royalty. It also symbolizes the need for preparation for the coming of Christ.

White — the purity of Jesus.

A white-birch log — symbolizes the manger and the cross.

The Red berries — symbolize the blood of Jesus shed for us.

The wreath should hold three purple and one rose candle. The rose candle is lighted on the third Sunday of Advent. The rose candle signifies joyfulness. It is often called the Joy candle.

On Christmas Eve the three purple and one rose candle should be removed. In their place four red candles should be inserted. At midnight, on Christmas Eve, one white candle is placed in the center of the wreath. This white candle is known as the Christ candle. It signifies the coming of Christ. The Christ candle should be lighted right at midnight.

First Candle — Prophecy Candle

Good morning and welcome. Today is the beginning of the Advent Season. It is the season of the Christian year when we make preparation for the birth of Jesus Christ. It is the season of promise and hope for all people. Let us start our preparation through these moments we now have together. "Prepare ye the way of the Lord, make straight a highway for our God."

On this first Sunday in Advent, Welcome! During the Advent Season there will be change in the worship experience; New faces, new candles and new songs. Advent is preparation for change and since the birth of Jesus the world has never been the same. May this Advent Season also change us as Christ is born anew in our lives and programs.

> **Minister:** Today is the beginning of Advent. The first candle we light is the **Prophecy** candle. It is a candle of hope and faith.

Lighting of the First Advent Candle.
> **Congregation:** Our first candle reminds us of our own faith in the goodness of God and the promise he made to his people long ago.

The words of the Prophet   Isaiah 7:14, 9:2-7

Unison Prayer

Hymn   "O Come, O Come Emmanuel"

Second Candle — Bethlehem Candle
Welcome to our worship service this second Sunday in Advent. During these days before Christmas we focus upon the concept of Incarnation. Incarnate is an unusual word which means "to invest with flesh or bodily nature and form." In the birth of Jesus, God takes on a "face" and becomes personified in Jesus, the Savior. In a similar way it is possible that God too, can become personified in us. That would be a wonderful gift at Christmas, to present God to others through us. Think about it!

Minister: This is the second Sunday of Advent. Let us prepare ourselves for Christ's birth.

Congregation: As we relight our first Advent candle, it reminds us of the promise God made to his people long ago and of faith in the goodness of God.

Minister: As we light the second candle, the Bethlehem Candle, let us remember Mary and Joseph journeying to Bethlehem and searching for a room where they could spend the night.

The News   Micah 5:2-4, Luke 2:1-7

Unison Prayer

Hymn   "O Little Town of Bethlehem"

Third Candle — The Shepherd's Candle
Good morning and welcome. We are now in the third Sunday of the Advent season. It is the season of the Christian year when we make preparation for the birth of Jesus Christ. This morning we light the rose candle,

which is symbolic of joyfulness and reminds us that Christmas is not far away. May we spend these moments together to prepare the way for "God with us".

    Minister: This is the third week of Advent and once again we relight our candles.

    Congregation: The first candle we light is the candle of Prophecy. As it is lighted we are reminded of the promise God made to his people long ago.

    Minister: As the second candle is lighted, let us remember Mary and Joseph journeying to Bethlehem searching for a room where they could spend the night.

    Congregation: The third candle reminds us of the announcement to the shepherds in the fields.

The Message to the Shepherds   Luke 2:8-20

Unison Prayer

Hymm   "Angels We Have Heard on High" or "Go Tell It on the Mountain" or "While Shepherds Watched their Flocks by Night"

The Fourth Candle — The Angel's Candle

Welcome to our worship service this fourth Sunday in Advent. Christmas is upon us! Even as we come to worship our minds are full of things yet to be done, activities to attend, and a lack of time to get ready. In these moments shared together, let us change our awareness from having Christmas come upon us, to having Jesus be born within us!

THE LIGHTING OF THE ADVENT CANDLES: FOURTH CANDLE

The Star and Angels' Candle

    Minister: This is the fourth Sunday of Advent. As we light the candles let us remember the meaning of each light.

People: The first candle is the Prophecy Candle. A hope come true as God gave his Son that we might have life. A faith built on the promises of God.

Minister: The second candle is a reminder of the love Mary and Joseph had for the Christ Child, a love we too can find.

People: The third candle is the angel's announcement of the birth of Jesus. May we be like the shepherds who heard the Good News and then shared it in joy and praise.

Minister: As we enter this last week of Advent, we light the fourth candle — a symbol of the star which led the wise men to Bethlehem.

People: So we too have found Christ and we also praise God today for our Lord Jesus.

Minister: Matthew 2:1-12

Unison Prayer

Hymn "Angels We Have Heard on High" or
"As With Gladness Men of Old"

Chrismon Tree

Why not have a Chrismon Tree this Christmas? The following service might give you some ideas. This service is designed to use six of your younger youth. Have three youth as shepherds and three youth as magi in costume. At the appropriate place in the service they could come forward and put symbols of what they represent on the tree. The Magi could bring their three gifts to put under the tree. During the offering have the youth remain and sit around the tree. During the anthem, they leave going their separate ways.

**THE LIGHTING OF THE CHRISMON TREE
THEME: "FROM DEITY TO HUMAN TO SAVE"**

Prelude   **Pianist**

*The Chiming of the Hour

*The Call to Worship

*The Hymn of Praise

*The Lighting of the Advent Candles

> **Minister:** In the beginning God said, "Let there be light; and there was light, and God saw that the light was good..." For centuries the good light of God guided the Hebrew people. To help explain God's act in the coming of the Christ, John opens his Gospel by saying: "In him was life, and the life was the light of men."
>
> **Congregation:** Light is one of the oldest and finest symbols man knows for God. In faith our fathers in the early church used lighted candles in a wreath to represent Advent, the season when one

prepares to receive anew the birth of the Christ. Thus we light the first and second candles in our Advent Wreath to remind us that the season of preparation moves toward fulfillment.

Minister: Jesus spoke to his disciples saying: "I am the light of the world . . . he who follows me . . . will have the light of life." Throughout the ages men have developed symbols that reminded them of the light of Jesus Christ.

Congregation: Our Chrismon Tree is lighted. It is our prayer that through the beauty of the tree, and through the symbols with which we decorate the tree, we may experience again the rebirth of the Christ in our souls and lives.

*The Invocation

The Greeting   Minister

The Sacrament of Communion [Optional]

*The Shepherd's Hymn

The Symbols of the Shepherds and Magi   Youth

The Message of the Shepherds

The Wise Men's Hymn   The Choir

The Message of the Wise Men

The Offering Sentence

Reception of Tithes and Offerings

Offering Dedication

The Anthem   The Choir

*The Benediction

*The Postlude

Project Nativity

Project Nativity can be set up in your annex the week before Christmas. This is a good way to get your youth active. You may also want to have a short movie and talk back stop.

PROJECT NATIVITY
A
WALK-THROUGH NATIVITY SCENE

In the next 30 minutes we hope that you will be reminded of the true meaning of Christmas. John described the significance of Jesus' birthday when he said: "God loved the world so much that he gave his only Son, so that anyone who trusts in him may never perish but have eternal life." (John 3:16)

PROJECT NATIVITY consists of five stops, each approximately four minutes long. The first four stops you will visit attempt to answer the following questions:
1. Why do I need Christmas?
2. Who is Jesus Christ?
3. What did Jesus do?
4. How does this affect me?

Please follow the directional signs to each of the stops. Your final stop will be the refreshment center.

STOP 1   **"FILM STOP"**
Slides and music reveal the coming of Christ in the midst of a troubled world. He is truly the Prince of Peace.

STOP 2   **"MINI-DRAMA STOP"**
Who is Jesus Christ?

STOP 3   **"PUPPET STOP"**
Puppets have always fascinated their audiences. They share with us the spirit of giving.

STOP 4   **"MUSIC STOP"**

STOP 5   **"REFRESHMENTS"**
We hope you have enjoyed your walk through Project Nativity. Enjoy a cookie with coffee or hot chocolate.

Hanging of the Greens

The Prelude

Lighting of the Candles

The Processional   "O Come All Ye Faithful"

The Call to Worship
> **Leader:** Arise, shine; for thy light is come, and the glory of the Lord is risen upon thee . . . Lift up thine eyes round about and see.
> **People: Sing and rejoice . . . for lo, I come, and I will dwell in the midst of thee, saith the Lord.**
> **Leader:** It is high time to awake out of sleep; for now is our salvation nearer than we had believed.
> **People: The night is far spent, the day is at hand; let us therefore cast off the works of darkness, and let us put on the armor of light.**
> **All: As with gladness men of old did the guiding star behold; as with joy they hailed its light, leading onward, beaming bright; so most gracious Lord may we evermore be led to thee.**
> **Leader:** (Prayer) O Loving Father, who has brought us again to the glad season when we commemorate the birth of thy Son, Jesus of Nazareth; open our hearts that we may joyfully welcome him to reign over us; open our lips that we too may sing with uplifted hearts, "Glory to God" in the highest, and on earth peace among men with whom he is pleased.

The Meaning of the Service

The Hanging of the Greens

The Chancel Greens
> The Scripture — Jeremiah 23:5-6

The Background
The Carol "Deck the Halls"

The Altar Greens
The Scripture — Luke 2:29-32
The Background
The Carol — "Away in a Manger"

The Lectern and Pulpit Greens
The Scripture — Isaiah 9:6-7
The Background
The Carol — "Hark the Herald Angels Sing"

The Sanctuary Greens
The Scripture — Luke 2:11-14
The Background
The Carol — "Birthday of a King"

The Litany for Advent
Leader: Prepare ye the way of the Lord; make straight in the desert a highway for our God.
People: And the Redeemer shall come to Zion, and unto them that turn from transgressions, saith the Lord.
Leader: Let us pray . . . Glory be to Thee Eternal God; thy glory shall be revealed and all flesh shall see it together; for thy mouth, O Lord, hath spoken it.
People: O Come, O Come, Immanuel.
Leader: Blessed art thou, O God of the prophets. Behold thou wilt come with a strong hand, and thy arm shall rule for thee.
People: Blessed be the King that cometh in the name of the Lord.
Leader: Thou shalt feed thy flock like a shepherd; thou shalt gather the lambs with thine arm, and carry them in thy bosom, and shall gently lead those that are with young.

People: **Blessed be he that cometh; peace in heaven and glory in the highest.**

Leader: (Prayer) Prepare our hearts, O God, for the coming of Jesus Christ, thy Son. Deepen our joy in making ready for the anniversary of his lowly birth at Bethlehem. By true faith in him, who is the desire of the nations, the promise of the prophets, the Prince of Peace, the Redeemer of men, may we rightly welcome him as the Savior of our souls and the Lord of our lives. Amen.

The Christmas Prayer

The Lighting of the Advent Candles
The Scripture — Isaiah 9:2, John 1:1-5,9
The Background
The Carol — "O Holy Night"

The Ringing of the Christmas Bells
Leader
The Scripture — Psalms 150
The Background
The Christmas Bells

The Benediction

The Recessional   "Joy to the World"

Postlude

Christmas Birthday Party

The following service was adapted from Dr. James L. Christensen's book "New Ways to Worship." This service is designed for Christmas Eve and allows for much congregational participation. You will need a large birthday cake, with twenty candles, on the communion table. Two small communion tables and two offering tray tables will be needed.

Each worshiper should be given a bulletin and a helium balloon as he arrives. Twenty worshipers should be given 3" x 5" cards with a contribution of Christ to read during the lighting of the birthday cake. The following could be adapted for Pentecost.

CHRISTMAS EVE

Birthday Celebration for Jesus

Music of Christmas　　　　　　　　　　　　　　　Organist

A Christmas Welcome and Call to Celebration

Processional Hymn　　　　　　"O Come All Ye Faithful"

Beginnings for Celebration:
  Minister: We have gathered to celebrate the birth of Jesus.
People: Thanks be to God for his gift.
  Minister: Jesus has come into our world through his birth; may we allow him to come into our lives through this worship experience.
  People: Yes, may the miracle of Christmas bring light into our world and lives.

Invocation

Lord's Prayer

Special Music   "Christmas Is A Birthday"

The Events Surrounding His Birth -   Luke and Matthew

Carol   "Silent Night! Holy Night"

A Christmas Litany
   Minister: For the lights of Christmas: for Christmas trees ablaze with light, colored lights in evergreen, and gleaming candles everywhere; for the story of the Christmas star and the bright stars in the winter sky —
   Congregation: Rejoice! Rejoice! Rejoice, give thanks and sing.
   Minister: For the music of Christmas: for the familiar carols and the organ music, for the story of the angels' song, and for Christmas bells ringing across the snow —
   Congregation: Rejoice! Rejoice! Rejoice, give thanks and sing.
   Minister: For the friendliness of Christmas: for Christmas cards of greeting and letters from friends far away, for family fun and fellowship, for visits and parties —
   Congregation: Rejoice! Rejoice! Rejoice, give thanks and sing.
   Minister: For the gifts of Christmas: for stockings filled with toys and goodies; mysterious, gay bundles; for secrets and surprises —
   Congregation: Rejoice! Rejoice! Rejoice, give thanks and sing.
   Minister: For the memory of Jesus, and for the love which his life and teaching brings into the world
   Congregation: Rejoice! Rejoice! Rejoice, give thanks and sing.

Carol   "Hark, The Herald Angels Sing"

The Sermon on Film   "The Very, Very, Very Best Christmas Present of All" (This is a must for the service)

Lighting of the Birthday Candles
Minister: Jesus has meant so much to our world — through his church and as a person. Let us recall some of his contributions that light up our world: (One candle is lit symbolizing a benefit for each century, since the birth of Jesus.) The people, (You) will chant just the **first** "Amen" of the "Great Amen." After each of the 20 candles is lit, we will sing all of the "Great Amen."

Communion Preparation

Meditation and Words of Institution

Presentation of Birthday Gifts Instructions: (Celebrator will come forward and place your offering in the offering plates and then proceed to the communion trays. Drink of the cup showing your individual relationship with God. Hold the bread for unison participation, that we might partake as a community. Finally, take your hymn book and form a large circle around the sanctuary.)

Words of invitation   Offertory Meditation

Offertory Prayer   Unison
O Lord, may these gifts we bring bless you Holy Name. May we find it to be a joyful experience to offer these gifts in the name of Jesus. We would desire to be like men of old who made offerings to Jesus. May we also leave singing praises to God.

presentation of Gifts (Congregation goes forward one person at a time from each side.)

Sharing the Lord's Supper
(Each celebrator serves himself at one of the communion tables, or can be served by the ministers, after placing an offering in the plates. **Drink** of the cup and **hold** the bread.)

Participation of the Bread
Chaplian: "This is my body which is broken for you, take and eat in rememberance of me."

Carol   "Joy to the World"

Benediction
Shalom and Merry Christmas (Celebrators are invited to the Fellowship Hall for Birthday Cake and refreshments.)

---

*Adapted from James L. Christensens **New Ways to Worship** p. 80

Christmas Eve Service

Prelude   "La Nativite"

Processional Hymn   "Joy to the World"

Invocation

Anthem   "Caroling, Caroling"

The Lighting of "The Christ Candle"
    The Four Candles of Advent
        The **Prophecy** Candle
        The **Bethlehem** Candle
        The **Shepherd's** Candle
        The **Angel's** Candle

The Call to Worship

A Service in Three Parts

Part I   **The Revelation to Shepherds**

Hymn   "While Shepherds Watched Their Flocks by Night"

Scripture Reading   Luke 2:8-20

Anthem   "All On A Christmas Morning"

Prayer

Meditation

Anthem   "For Jesus Christ is Born"

Part II   **The Visit By Wise Men**

Hymn   "As With Gladness Men of Old"

Scripture Reading   Matthew 1:18 - 2:12

Anthem   "Mary Had a Baby"

Prayer

Meditation

Hymn   "O Little Town of Bethlehem"

Part III   **Our Response to Christmas**

Worship Leader

The Christmas Eve Offering for Benevolence

Offertory   "Silent Night

The Affirmation   (In Unison with All Standing)
We confess that Jesus is the Christ, the Son of the Living God, and proclaim him Lord and Savior of the world.

In his name and by his grace we accept our mission of witness and service to mankind.

We rejoice in God our Father, maker of heaven and earth, and in the covenant of love by which he has bound us to himself.

Through baptism into Christ we enter into newness of life and are made one with the whole people of God.

In the fellowship and communion of Holy Spirit we are joined to one another in brotherhood and in obedience to Christ.

At the table of the Lord we celebrate with

thanksgiving his saving acts and his presence.

Within the universal church we receive the gift of ministry and the light of Scripture.

In the bonds of Christian faith we yield ourselves to God, that we may serve him whose kingdom has no end.

Blessing, glory, and honor be to him forever. Amen.

The Litany of Re-Dedication

Leader: Speak to us of love at Christmas, O God!

Congregation: Love that is warm, sincere, and ever living! Love that is the practical answer to the world's problems. Love that finds expression in a friendly concern for our neighbors, in a just give-and-take in the market-place, in a firm devotion to clean thinking and right acting.

Leader: Speak to us of joy, at Christmastime, O God!

Congregation: Joy that is vibrant, wholesome, and contagious! Joy that is able to change a frown to a smile. Joy that has its roots in self-denial, a faithful adherence to goodness, and in a Christian concern for others.

Leader: Speak to us of peace, at Christmastime, O God!

Congregation: Peace that is universal, yet individual; peace that is outward, yet inward first. Peace that is a natural development among men of goodwill.

Leader: Speak to us of Christ, at Christmastime, O God!

Congregation: The Christ who himself was love, joy, and peace! The Christ who is able to give light to them that sit in darkness and in the shadow of death; who is able to guide our feet in the way of peace.

Leader: "God so loved the world that he gave his only Son, that whoever believes in him shall not perish, but have everlasting life."

> Congregation: In thankful acknowledgement of God's Divine Onwership of life and the world, and in grateful recognition of his gifts entrusted to us, we, his people, this Christmas Eve, do give unto him, such as we are and have.
>
> Leader: "Jesus said, 'I am come that they might have life, and have it abundantly ... I am the way, the truth, and the life."
>
> Congregation: In sincere appreciation of the practical and life-giving ministry of Jesus we remember the work which Christmas begins: to find the lost, to heal the broken, to feed the hungry, to release the prisoner, to rebuild the nations, to bring peace among brothers, to make music in the heart.
>
> Leader: As the Wise Men presented their gifts and were led to him who alone is worthy of the adoration and love of mankind, may the Christmas love of God give new birth to Christians here and everywhere to the end that the light that was born that night so long ago in Bethlehem may continue to shine.
>
> Congregation: O God, help us now and ever as thy people to be "the light of the world."

Hymn   "O Come All Ye Faithful"

Benediction

Combined Choirs   "Hallelujah Chorus"
Handel

Postlude   "O Come All Ye Faithful"

Candlelight Service

Christmas Eve candlelight and communion services are becoming very popular. The following is an adapted service. It should start in total light. A candle is lighted for each light celebrated. During the "light in me" section you should turn off all of the lights so that only the Advent candles and eight light candles are visible. At midnight light the Christ Candle.

CHRISTMAS EVE CANDLELIGHT AND COMMUNION SERVICE

God quietly entered human history on a night such as this, and the world was changed. Tonight we celebrate this event called Christmas, not so much to re-enact a historical event, but to experience his birth in us. So we pray, "Come again Lord Jesus. May our symbols, songs and words bring birth to you again, this time in our own personal worlds. Amen."

The Prelude

The Processional   Choir
"Prepare Ye, The Way of The Lord"

The Lighting of the Advent Wreath
The Prophecy Candle   The Shepherd's Candle

The Bethlehem Candle   The Angel's Candle

The Choral Call to Worship   "O Come, All Ye Faithful"

The Light of Hope
Words of Scripture   Isaiah 9:2

Words of Celebration

The Carol of Hope   "Come, Thou Long Expected Jesus"

The Light of Faith
Words of Scripture   Luke 2:1-7

Words of Celebration

The Carol of Faith   "Gesu Bambino"

The Light of Joy
Words of Scripture   Luke 2:8-14

Words of Celebration   (In Unison)

The Carol of Joy   "Joy To The World"

The Light of Wonder
Words of Scripture   Luke 2:15-20

Words of Celebration

The Carol of Wonder   "I Wonder as I Wander"

The Light of Gratitude
Words of Scripture   Luke 2:15-20

Words of Celebration

The Carol of Peace "It Came Upon the Midnight Clear"

The Light of Incarnation
Words of Scripture   John 1:1-5, 10-14

Words of Celebration
       We celebrate the fact that God's Glory became flesh in Jesus and that the disciples saw the glory of

the only Son of the heavenly Father, so we could see Jesus even as they saw him.

The Meditation "Incarnation in the Lord's Supper"

Words of Invitation and Institution

A Prayer of Confession
We do not come to this communion table, our Father, trusting in ourselves. We know that whenever we try to be our own gods, we become confused and lost. We come this Christmas Eve because we have reached the conclusion that the only way for us to really live is by trusting in you and allowing you to be free. so, we humble ourselves before you, and we confess our sins and our need for you. May our participation in this Lord's Supper allow you to be "with us" as you choose; may it remind us that we are your community, and may it lead us to the mangers of our modern world where you are alive, to the silent nights and sights where your glory is known, to the humble places where you are honored. Amen.

The Light in Me
Words of Scripture   John 8:12, Matthew 5:14-16

Words of Celebration   (In Unison)
We celebrate the fact that Christ came to bring new life to us, and that we might have this light of life within us; we continue our celebration as we go forth with our lives aglow with the spirit of Christ, challenging us to reflect him through our thoughts, words, and deeds.

The Carol of Light   "Silent Night, Holy Night
(In the darkness come to the altar and light your candle from the Christ Candle and return to your place, coming one row at a time, until everyone's light is shining through the darkness.)

A Christmas Prayer

Father

It is **good** to be here and to feel your presence among us. All we have to do is **ask** and you respond. Hear our prayers! We know that each may approach you in his own way. Hear not only words which are audible, but hear those **concerns** and **joys** which are on every mind.

This is a special time of the year for us. We **anticipate** and **celebrate** the birth of Jesus, your **son**, our **Lord and Savior**. The advent wreath tells us that that time is very near. About this event we come singing **songs** and **carols**.

To all Christians we **beckon**, "O Come All Ye Faithful," and like the Herald Angels we sing, "**Glory to the Newborn King.**"

However, what we sing about is not always to be found in our world.

FOR

1. All is not calm and bright in the silent night.
2. Peace on the earth, and good will to men is not a reality.
3. We sing joy to the world the Lord is come, let the earth receive her king, **but** every heart does not sing the praises of Jesus.
4. Away in a manger there is no room for a babe; this is also true of many hearts.

Help make these words realities, for they speak of your kingdom which was **begun** with the birth of Christ and which is to **come** in its fullness.

Do you hear what I hear?
1. I hear dreams of a white Christmas.
2. I hear glory to the newborn king.
3. We, like the new bird, would sing a love song as we go along.

4. I hear silver bells and declare that it is Christmas in this city.
5. People are passing, children are laughing, showing smile after smile.

This Christmas season brings visions of **mistletoe, Frosty the Snowman,** and **Santa Claus.**

We would pray for:
The **caring** which is found under the mistletoe,
The desire to come **alive** found in Frosty,
The desire to **give** which is found in Santa.

Mostly we remember the reality that Jesus Christ is what Christmas is all about. It is about him that we sing. Help us to give Christ his rightful place during his season. As the silent night comes, may he become the light of our world.

May we, like the three kings, follow that star of wonder, star of night, and star of royal beauty bright that it may guide us by its perfect light. That we might know the wonders of his love.

> In the name of Jesus
> In the presence of the spirit
> And in the love of God
> Amen.

Live Nativity

A most meaningful experience, for any church, is to have a live nativity scene during the week before Christmas. Many churches have built elaborate scenes. What follows is a very inexpensive and simple scene. It should take six to eight men three hours to complete all of the work. Your cost should run about $100.

You would need the following materials:
- 4 - 3" x 8' poles
- 6 - 8 ft. 2 x 4
- 6 - 10 ft. 2 x 4
- 8 - 12 ft. 2 x 4
- 3 - Panels
- 40 ft. - 4' x 2" Chicken Wire
- 14 - 2" x 6½' poles
- Gate material, backing for manger, lights — 4-5 spots will do
- At least one donkey
- 2 goats and 2 sheep

The ladies of the church can make simple costumes for:
— Mary, Joseph, a plastic baby can be used for Baby Jesus, 3 wisemen, 3 shepherds, and two angels.

Now you will need to record a tape to use for the action. The following represents a tape that contained five minutes of prelude and postlude music. It then tells the Christmas story in words and music for fifteen additional minutes.

Prelude   Medley
("Joy to the World," "Sing We Now," "O Tannenbaum," "O Holy Night")

Isaiah 9:6-7c   spoken over the music of "Silent Night"

Luke 2:1-4   (Pause) Over the music of "O Little Town of Bethlehem"

"Away in a Manger" — words of the song only

Matthew 2:1-10, 2:11-12 — (10 second pause; over the music of "We Three Kings"

Luke 2:8-10   No Music

Man's voice   10 - 12

Luke 2:13

Several voices   2:14

Jazzy verson of "Hark the Herald Angels Sing"

Luke 2:15-20 — over the music of "O Come All Ye Faithful"

Postlude: "What Child is This" by Julie Andrews and "Joy to the World" by the Robert Shaw corale.

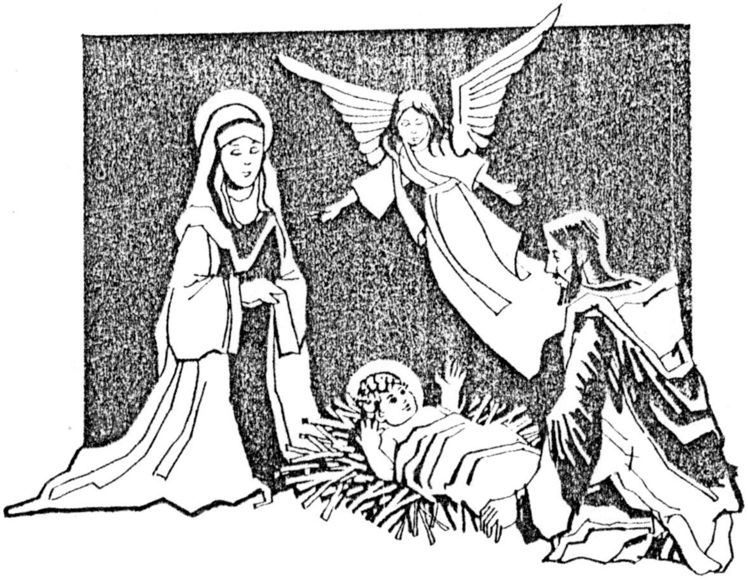

A Maundy Thursday Service

Maundy Thursday is a good time for a special service. A reproduction of the Last Supper can be a very meaningful experience for any congregation. This presents an opportunity for thirteen of your men to get together.

The evening starts out with a short serice. The Last Supper reproduction follows. The men will sit down to eat a real Passover meal. Your service could end with a candle light communion service in your fellowship hall. Tables could be arranged with thirteen chairs at each table. Let the men who played the Disciple roles serve the communion to their table, if your tradition allows. A suggested service and script follow.

Prelude   Organist

Call to Celebration

Hymn of Gathering and Praise   "We Gather Together"

A Welcome

The Good News   Matthew 26:17-30

Pastoral Prayer

Hymn of Preparation   "Let Us Break Bread Together"

The Presentation
    Place: Upper room in Jerusalem
    Time: The Thursday of his betrayal

Communion Service

The Benediction

Live Last Supper

Introduction

The whole week, of which the Passover Feast occupied the first evening, was called the Feast of Unleavened Bread.

This feast commemorated the greatest event in the history of Israel: The deliverance from slavery in Egypt. All Jews were required to celebrate this fest within the boundaries of the city.

Jesus and his twelve Apostles came to Jerusalem to celebrate the Passover Feast. At this common meal the leader recalls to the participants the mighty acts of God in their earlier national history. It was in such a context that Jesus deliberately introduced a new element into the ancient liturgy, transforming it into the Lord's Supper.

Accounts of this feast are found in Matthew 26, Mark 14, Luke 22, and 1 Corinthians 11. Let us now join Jesus and his Apostles, found in Matthew 26:17-30, as they celebrate the Passover.

Jesus.................	Bartholomew...........
Peter.................	Thomas...............
John	Andrew ....
Thaddaeus	Matthew..............
Judas	James A. ....
James	Simon ....
Philip	

(Only Peter and John enter from the side and they spontaneously talk about their walk until they get to the table.)

Peter: You know, John, that sure was easy. All we had to do was say: "The teacher says my hour has come; my Disciples and I will celebrate the Passover at your house", and we were shown to this upper room. It was just as Jesus said.

John: The Master must have arranged that password with his friend at an earlier date. Peter, I do wonder what the others are doing while we are here. I hope we don't miss anything.

Peter: We had better get busy with the preparations for the Passover Feast. (looking around) Let's see! Looks like our host has prepared the unleavened bread and has rid the house of leavened bread.

John: How about the lamb? I do not see one up here. (looking around) I hope that our host took the lamb to the temple for us.

Peter: Let me go check and see. (Leave through the door entered)

John: (thinks out loud) I wonder why the Master sent me for such a petty job, when he could have sent someone else. What's so special about **this** particular meal anyway? Jesus has been strange today. He has been talking about being handed over to be nailed on a cross and talking about some final judgement. Boy, I just don't understand. I guess the Master will explain more at tonight's celebration.

Peter: (enter with a lamb on a plate) OK, the lamb has been slain and the blood offered to God as a sacrifice. (put lamb on table) Let's see what else we need to prepare.

John: Peter, how about you pouring the four cups of wine and being sure that there is salt water in each bowl.

Peter: OK, then you gather the herbs and mix the paste.

John: Right!

Peter: Looks like all of the ingredients are close at hand. Our host seems to have made available just about everything we need. Here are the bowls of salt water which remind us of the tears shed while slaves in Egypt and of the Red Sea through which our people escaped.

John: Here are the herbs which remind us of the bitterness of slavery. This paste reminds us of days that our fathers were compelled to make bricks in Egypt. These sticks of cinnamon will represent the straw with which the bricks were made.

Peter: Lastly the four cups of wine as reminder of the four promises God promised our people: (pour cup, and then give the promise it symbolizes)
1. I will bring you out from under the burdens of the Egyptians.
2. I will rid you of the bondage.
3. I will redeem you with an outstretched arm.
4. I will take you to me for a people, and I will be your God.

John: Looks like we are almost ready and it's getting dark. It sounds like people are coming up the stairs. (Disciples make walking noises)

Peter: (looking around) Hey brothers, where is the Master? (Disciples move in front of table)

James: The Master has gone apart to pray for a while. He seemed to be troubled about something.

Thomas: Yes, he keeps talking about his death and it scares me. At least we won't hear anymore about that at tonight's celebration.

Thaddaeus: While you were talking with Thomas, I got to thinking that we are a strange bunch that Jesus called. Each of us is so different. Peter and Andrew were fishermen. James and John were fishermen . . .

Philip: I was also a fisherman.

Barth: And I was a herdsman.

Thadaeus: And Matthew, you were a tax collector.

James [A]: Christ even called Simon here, who was a Zealot (pat on shoulder)

Thaddaeus: And you, Judas, were a businessman.

Judas: Right. And a shrewed one at that.

Thaddaeus: We may have all come from differing backgrounds, but we have been through a lot together. We have a lot of memories.

Talk about teaching ... "I remember"
(Three Disciples in each group, each group speaks once and in order, groups should stand together.)
    Calm Storm — walk on water
    Sermon on the Mount — Lord's Prayer
    Healings — Greatest Command
    Feeding 5,000

Andrew: (Needs to be in group No. 1; then goes to window, keeps looking out window and says little. After the last group is through, Andrew says:) "Here comes Jesus."

Jesus: (Enters) The streets are crowded. There is an air of expectation outside.

Have a seat brothers. Let us experience the love of God as we celebrate the Passover.
- A. All are seated
- B. The lamb is passed by Jesus to each side
- C. Dip fingers into the salt water and put to lips
- D. Herbs and paste are passed — small amount on plate
- E. Each Disciple should engage in spontaneous conversation during the meal.
- F. Jesus lifts up a loaf of unleavened bread.

"This is the bread of affliction which our fathers ate in the land of Egypt. Let everyone who hungers come and eat; let everyone who is in need come and eat the Passover meal." (The bread is put down unbroken. Each disciple takes a bite from his own cracker — dips another piece in one of the four cups; one is on each table. Eat 1-2 minutes)

"Truly, I say to you, one of you will betray me."

Disciples: (Each asks spontaneously — except Judas:) "Is it I, Lord?"

Jesus: He who dipped his hand in the dish with me, will betray me. The Son of Man goes as it is written of him; but woe to that man by whom the

Son of Man is betrayed! It would be better for that man if he had not been born.

Judas: Is it I, Master?

Jesus: You have said so. (Eat 1-2 minutes). Takes bread, puts hand over bread and looks upward for 5-10 seconds; breaks bread — 1/2 to each side)

Brothers, take off a piece as it comes your way.

(After all are served) "This is my body which is broken for you. Take and eat in rememberance of me." (All look puzzled — eat of bread — finish eating)

(Jesus lifts his cup of wine) "Praised art thou, O Lord our God, king of the universe, who has created the fruit of the vine." (All drink from their cups; table talk for 1-2 minutes — holds hand over the cup and looks up for 5-10 seconds)

"Drink of it all of you; for this is my blood of the covenent, which is poured out for many for the forgiveness of sins. I tell you that I shall not drink again of this fruit of the vine until that day when I drink it new with you in my Father's Kingdom." (Each drinks from his cup) (All sit and stare at Jesus, looking puzzled; tension builds)

Simon: (Looks tense) oooh! (hit stomach), that was a good meal.

Philip: It makes one mindful of the wonders of God. If it were not for God and his mighty acts, our people may never have gotten out of Egypt.

Matthew: Praise God!

James [A]:

Barth: AMEN

Jesus: Glory and thanks be to God.

Andrew: AMEN BROTHER

Matthew: Jesus, what did you mean when you broke bread and said it was your body broken for us? I don't understand.

Simon: And what were the new words that you said over the cup of blessing?

Barth: Yes, I don't understand either one Lord.
Jesus: Brothers, you may not now understand what has happened, but remember my words and actions. For tonight a new covenant has been established. When you gather together, you are to partake of these vessels of commemoration and forgiveness. You will partake of them in remembrance of me, for I shall only be with you a short while longer. We have just remembered the Father's mighty acts in Egypt with this passover supper. This new institution will celebrate what I will do for you very shortly.
Andrew: What do you mean?
James [A]: What will you do?
Peter: Recently, you keep talking about your death. Is that what you are talking about?
Jesus: (Pause) We have been here too long; let us be off to the Mount of Olives. (all leave with Jesus leading the way)

END

Lent Suggestions

1. Have your church members write a devotional book for use during Lent. Ask each family to write one or two devotions. Combine these devotions into a book for your congregation. These devotions are to be read from Ash Wednesday until Easter. This project allows for sharing and community building.

2. If you are in the right situation you might want to try a Lenten luncheon or supper once a week during the season of Lent. I would suggest a twenty minute service and a meal. Guest ministers could be invited to speak. You could use filmstrips or a big worship banner. A good idea is to add a different symbol of Holy Week to a banner each week that you meet. You a might even want to add the final figure of an empty cross as part of your Easter worship experience.

EASTER CAROLING

Easter caroling may be a new experience for your church to try. Meet at the church on the Saturday night before Easter Sunday. Pass out a sheet of mimeographed words to each participant. I might suggest that your Easter caroling be directed toward the workers in your church. This would be a good way to let your workers know that they are very much appreciated.

After caroling, you may want to go to a home and dye eggs and decorate baskets to be given to the Sunday school children in the morning. You might be surprised at the results that you get from Easter caroling.

PARISH PARTY

It sure is hard to meet all of the members when you move into a new church. Why not try a Parish Party? You could invite groups of ten or twelve people over to the parsonage for the purpose of getting to know each other. This would be a quick way to meet your new congregation. This method might get people interested that have not been active for some time. When you call on people it is not uncommon to find that they are not at home. This is not a problem if things are at your home. Parish parties allow for quicker acquaintances and let you know about the needs of your new congregation.

MUSIC IDEAS

1. Sing "Amazing Grace" to the tune of "I Would Love to Teach the World to Sing"
2. Sing the Doxology to the tune of:
   A. Gloria (Latin style)
   B. All Creatures of Our God and King
3. Have a hymn of the month that you learn by singing it at every worship service that month.
4. After the Doxology sing the last verse of America.

Children's Easter Sermon

Have the younger children come up and sit on the steps. Begin by asking them what are some of the symbols of Easter. Now ask the kids if they know why Easter is on a different date each year. If there is no answer then you might want to try the congregation. If you have no luck you might explain that Easter is the first Sunday after the first full moon after March 21. Easter can range from 21 March to 25 April. The minister can then explain that the bunny was an ancient symbol of the moon. The moon and bunnies are both related to Easter.

At this point you should ask the groups about the reason for Easter eggs. If no answers, explain that eggs used to be placed on the coffins of loved ones. The thought was that their loved ones would come out of the shell of their dead body much like the way that a baby comes out of the shell of an egg. Thus eggs are symbols of eternal life.

Since you have talked about eggs and bunnies it would be appropriate to give each child a bunny or an egg to take back to the pew.

Benedictions

Grant us thy peace, as now we go our way, with thee began, with Thee shall end the day. Guard thou the lips from sin, the heart from shame, that in this house have called upon Thy name. AMEN

Minister: Let not the existence of evil in the world persuade you that life is finished. With singing and dancing, caring and loving, be in the world a presence that is alive to life.
People: We are the ones who bring the mark of the new life in Christ. We shall be as reconciliation, peace, mercy, and love in the world.

Go into the world in peace. As you go, look outward toward your fellow man. As you go, look inward to find God who will undergird your faith. Go now seeker and search his ways. AMEN

Go now in peace. Leave to discover and express who God is, who you are, and who we are as a Christian community. Now may the Lord watch between me and thee while we are absent one from another. AMEN.